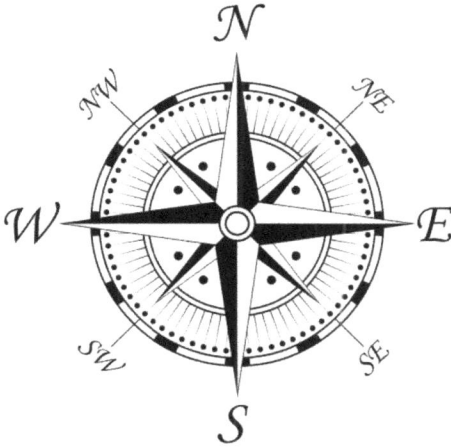

22

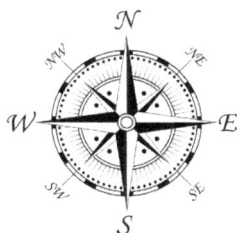

a collection of poetry
gigi bella

"The reflection of the '2' is his identity bound up in duality: the relationship he has with himself and the relationship he has with the rest of the world. 'A Million' is the rest of that world: the millions of people we will never know, the infinite and endless, everything outside of one's self that makes you who you are. '22, A Million' is thus part love letter, part final resting place of searching for self-understanding like a religion. And an inner-resolution of maybe never finding that understanding."

-Trevor Hagen referring to Bon Iver's "22, A Million"

{ON THE COMPONENTS OF SELF}

{ON WOMANHOOD}

{ON LOVE}

{ON SURVIVAL}

{ON THE COMPONENTS OF SELF}

{GRINGA}

When I was small,
my mother called me
        Ginger.
The neighborhood show tune and shimmer,
glam and glitter
like cookie dust rubbed strong war paint on my cheeks
A freckled pancake of my mother's lip gloss and bronzer
My eyes,
a serious brown above my butterfly net of a nose

All because I stopped to smell the roses too many times
A sniff of smoke
fluttering from my Granny's 99 cent saint candles
Wax Jesus
whispering the rip off Frida Kahlo's
on my grandmother's walls
Her Sunday morning hymn to the television priest
floating-
I always wondered why he sung all of his sermons
As if they would reach the heavens quicker
Quicker than the smell of arroz y frijoles
down the hallway to my bedroom door
Like fast fingers penning my name to paper
just minutes after I was born
                white sugar
that tasted like a beach sand brown
I once dated a boy who called me
                white sugar
Said he liked the way my legs were like fresh snow
What he didn't know is that

every time he compared me to winter
I became a seething summer,
my skin, a rippling rage
Every time I'd say,
       "I'm not white"
and he'd laugh and say, "right"
When I was small my mother called me
       Ginger
and the rest of the world mispronounced me
until my name became
       Gringa.
White washed, Cultural shame
And I can show them my birth certificate
and tell them my name
but I will still be face to face
with girls who look just like my cousins
Their parents like my ninos and ninas
not understanding that I was once a niña just like them
       No pinche puta poser
They speak Spanish because they know I won't understand
It's not my fault
the universe wrote a letter to my mother's womb
and said they'd like me better
if my name and my skin didn't match
Said they'd be more proud
if my tongue stayed in one piece
I am tired of being identified as a traitor
for secrets I didn't share
because I walk down the street being judged
for the color of my hair
"No way she's Hispanic"
       "Does she think we're stupid?"
   "White girls don't even know what brown looks like."

But none of these accusations have seen my insides
My barrio blood coursing through peacock feather venas;
adobe aorta
Each ventricle filled with the smell of green chile
and a mother singing from the kitchen
Sangre de mi Sangre, dejadme en el olvido
   Sangre de mi Sangre
      Blood of my blood
Leave me in oblivion
because you've forgotten all of the children who don't
look exactly like you
I will never understand why
I am not allowed to be one of your people
My name is
 GABRIELA ESPERANZA YOLANDA GUAJARDO
They call my skin
   GiGi
They call my writing
   Gringa
When I was small, my mother called me
   Ginger

{FOUR}

There's this little girl.
She is 4 years old and sticky with glitter and life
and fresh peanut butter and jelly
She has at least 2 questions for every coiled ribbon of hair
on her head
She is tutus and ruby red slippers
Dreams of television set stardom and cotton candy castles
She is her own sunshine and limelight
Her own sweet lemonade and plastic purple high heels
She is

so

very

f o u r
I ask her what she wants to be when she grows up
She answers,
"a rockstar princess fairy....queen!"
and all I can think is
Why isn't there a degree for that?
Why can't I have a BA in Unicorn Studies?
Why isn't there a lab where you learn
how to make glitter and ball gowns?
What ever happened to being whatever you want when
you grow up?
I want to ban the word dream
and make everything a reality
There is nothing too far away; nothing too crazy
We'll be Batman doctors and astronaut pirates!
Beyonce, first woman president of the United States
and Harry Potter, Nascar champion!
We'll pave our streets with Legos

and build our houses with Lincoln Logs
There will be a firework show outside our window
every night
We will never once have to change our major because
We will have everything we ever wanted
All of our stardust scattered along the galaxy
like a trail of breadcrumbs
leading us back when we get lost
When we finally do grow up, we'll live in a world
where teachers get paid the same
as the people who make all the rules
and there's no such thing as cutting creativity out of
education
because creativity is the education
Where artists can live off of their creation
and poets can live off of their wisdom
without back-ups schemes or plan b's
We're the O.G.'s of dreaming like it's kindergarten
all over again
Hell, I'm 22 years old and still waiting for the day
I wake up with a mermaid tail
because I never stopped dreaming
I never stopped being
so
very
F o u r
Just like her,
all Hopscotch shimmy and butterfly sing-song
Because let's face it, being a grown up…
fucking sucks
but being Spider-Man or Super Mom
or whatever you were meant to be
that's what life's about

{DADDY'S GIRL}

I've always been under the impression
my childhood was normal
because no one ever told me otherwise
Nobody pulled me by the buns and said
"Hey…
you realize your dad's the dark lord of the galaxy right?"
I mean, he never mentioned that shit at career day
Didn't sit me down over our favorite cereal
to tell me who he was off to destroy
He loved his girl and his boy
Luke and Leia, pride and joy,
our childhood was the intergalactic bomb
because my dad was totally THAT guy
Who claimed the sock bun was an abomination
and invented an entire machine
just to put my hair up the same every day
Had my white outfits dry cleaned by droids
I was Vader's little princess,
Daddy's little destroyer
and he promised himself that he'd raise me to be
the baddest bitch this side of Tattoine
Everybody thinks that he's just another bad guy
but I gotta come to terms with the fact
he did all this for me
so every male in this universe would see that
nobody was gonna fuck with his daughter
My definition of Star Wars was bringing boys home
Dinners where we'd sit twiddling our thumbs
Listening to father breathe
Chh—ha-chh-ha-chh-haa

My hottie super bomb Solo would start to speak
and daddy would just stand up and thrust his grip forward
as my date levitated while turning purple
and dad would just say
"What is it, son, force got your tongue?"
I was pretty sure he'd never talk to me again
because my Dad never let me have boyfriends
Which brings me to the time
I fell in love with my brother…
Maybe it's a cause and effect type thing?
Despite my Dad's unconventional ways,
there was this side of him the world never knew
because I remembered him as the galactoid grill master
Our barbecues were the SITH!
He made grub better than the Cantina,
Jabba would've approved
I'll never forget the way his apron hung around his neck
like a second cape
that read:
"Kiss the dark lord"
across the front pocket
Equipped with his matching chef hat,
I hate that no one else has ever heard him laugh
No one's ever felt a Vader hug
I'll never forget the moment that broke me in half
The day that daddy found me in my college years
Crazy shit happens at Jedi University,
and all those hunky warriors in training wanted
a piece of me
Just that girl with the hot buns from Kappa Wookie
Suddenly I was that gold bikini'd space skank
plastered on every frat house wall
The cover of Planet Boy magazine

proudly screaming my name over my gold lamé ass cheeks
Dad never thought he'd open our teleported mail to that
I could feel the disappointment through his mask
as he trudged out
"You have failed me for the last time"
and hung up… like an explosion of my dwarf star heart
I know we're gonna meet again some day
so I can tell him that I'm still his little girl
Despite the fact that everyone I know tells me
that he didn't even know he had a daughter,
I refuse to believe the lie!
Because even though all of these memories are
a little blurry,
I know he has them too…

I love you, Darth Daddy

As I sit here sorting this out in my therapist's office
all I can say is
Help me, Pops,

You're my only hope

{HOW TO FREE A CAGED TONGUE}

After Gloria Anzaldua.

I remember the first time I realized
not everyone's grandma referred to them as *mijita*
The time I figured out that pelicula meant
we were going to the movies
Because surprises were spoken of in Spanish
Between Mama and Mima
To keep quiet and secret
Sacred and silent
Their language of Christmas presents and shit-talk
I could color code you a map of my Burque
Beginning with Nino and Nina
Bathed in cigarette smoke and crushed Pepsi cans
Granny at the table,
her forked tongue silent beneath her loud Catholic mouth
My grandmother had two funerals

     Mass

My first vision of La Virgen
Knees imprinted purple
The priest prayed in Español
Beads counted
    1.   What am I doing here?
    2.   I don't understand
    3.   This is no place for tear-stained ginger girls
I wondered if this was meant to be
a secret kept from me too
Silent and sacred
The apple dangled in front of Eve
My native tongue cut out

and running away from my own mouth
We only just caught up with each other
And she said call me Malinche
Traitor,
       pocha,
              la chingada
I am middleman and mestiza
I am making you see stars, double vision,
before I come together
I am Gringa by day
Before the blue corn moon turns me into…
Super Chicana!
Here to save the day con la revolucion
And my Mima's green chile chicken enchiladas
Gloria Anzaldua and I should have coffee and biscochitos
And talk about pochismos
She sounds like my cool auntie with all that she taught me
Serpent tongue and the revocation of silence
The woman,
      the poet,
           the chicana
Rewrite me, though I was never wrong
Unbreakably mixed, mutt, mestiza
Let me reclaim you
Upgrade you from what I thought I'd never have
to who I'm proud to be
Me
Surrendering my shame and remembering my names
          All of them
Call me
Mestiza Malinche
      Or pinche pocha
         Gringa

Chingada
　　Chicana
　　　　Mujer de colores

Free and untamed
This way I will remain
Despite those who spray paint me sellout,
cross out my eyes and silence my tongue
Young and impenetrable
When they use my Spanish for target practice,
I will tell them that this is the new dance of my syllables
The siren song of my pride
When they place skin beside skin
I will tell them that the revolution
comes in more than one color
This is our reclamation
Our beating drum and matching march
This is where colorblind falls in love with twenty-twenty
and they birth hindsight
This is the moment where we stop being separate
Stop trying to stay one rung above each other
on life's ladder
This is where we remix till we sing together seamlessly
And it will sound like Selena instead of cochina
It will sound like dreaming instead of divisive scheming
It will sound like the birth of two tongues
left wild and unruly
And we will never be able to stop listening.

{SLUT}

Seventh grade never taught me that I'd like sex
because everything was an STD or cartoon pornography
The closest we got to feeling anything
was the time we had to feel up those beanbag testicles
to check for cancer
There was nothing appealing about
Mrs. Henry's plastic vagina
Nothing glorious about its male companion so aptly named
"Woody"
They never taught me just how hard it would be
Because seventh grade taught me that if I liked sex,
I'd earn myself a new name:
  S L U T
The girl who doesn't see the logic in
sleeping on top of the sheets
when you could be between them
The girl who's talented by day
and even more talented by night
The girl who was always badass at flying kites
because she knows exactly how to get things up
They call me
  SLUT
because I like the way my own orgasms sound
and every month when it's time for my period I'm like
"Hi. Can this be done now?
'Cause my coochie's got places to be"
Because you haven't met good sex until you've met me
I'm that girl you don't expect
Learned my lessons from Lollabrigida and Monroe
    I smell sex and candy, yeahhh....

They call me
        SLUT
because I love being told I'm sexy
but it doesn't really seem like anyone's with me
when they call me slut...
like a nasty assumption that hangs on their lips
every time they say they'll pray for me
Because suddenly, I'm the prom queen of promiscuity,
an STD leper,
no one can talk to me or I'll breathe herpes and hell fire
They call ME slut to get away from the fact that they're
afraid of their own sexuality
Yeah, I like freaky weekends
and boys who know a good time
but that doesn't mean I've completely lost my mind
I know safety like seatbelts,
look at promiscuity like a poster of the girl I'm not
Just because I like sex doesn't mean I'm having it with
everything with a dick,
        DICK!
Give the women of this day and age a little credit
because I'm straight up Carrie Bradshaw
but this country treats me like I'm 16 and pregnant
I'm entitled to my own choices
yet the government wants to march into my downstairs
and make me listen to their damn voices
Don't try to tell me my precautions aren't good enough
because birth control is my best friend
If pills are for sluts
Then call me
        SLUT
Because I know who I am and I know what I like
      and we shouldn't be taught to fear our own bodies

Because I love the way my skin hugs my bones
I'm not afraid of the image I see
straight out of the shower
        Don't you see that we are beauty?
I'm not afraid of beautiful things
So call me SLUT
because I love knowing that I fit in somewhere
Call me SLUT,
because I make love with more passion than you
Call me SLUT
because my vagina is fucking magnificent
and I may not be married to the guy
but I deserve a good rodgering every once in a while
        So do yourself a favor,
be proud of who you are
and how fucking sexy God made you
and in the name of all things that are good
        GET LAID TONIGHT

{ON WOMANHOOD}

{WAR PAINT}

My favorite lipstick is a technicolor indigo prism purple
The kind of color that makes a 3-D movie out of my lips
My lips are a neon open sign
They are never closed and always have something to say
Boys say purple lipstick is for alien girl weirdos
who long to be unacceptable
That they will not give in to a color
that their limited male gaze does not approve
They refuse to be kissed by something different
These same boys will call us queens of deception
With our contour and porcelain and pretty
They will watch us at the bathroom mirror and say
"You don't have to wear all that makeup for me,"
And the first thought in my head is
Hey, asshole, who the fuck said I was doing this for you?
You don't even know the difference between
Wet n' Wild and Kat Von D
The pure victory of perfect winged eyeliner
that didn't happen
Three hours and seventeen make-up wipes later
That Beyonce, "Flawless," "I woke up like this," feeling
we dreamt of as little girls
watching our mothers put on lipstick for the first time
Calling it sanctuary
This female face is sacred in a world where nothing else is
There is so little we get to control
This is prayer, a parable written for every part of me
My nose, my cheeks, my lips, my eyebrows
My eyelashes
that stretch to the top of the Sandia Mountains

Revealing the Burque sunset that lives in my eyes
Call me gospel
This is ritual with every brush and stroke
You wanna know how I got this look?
I learned how to glow up from Artemis herself!
Call me goddess of the battlefield because *I slay*
This isn't child's play,
this is motherfuckin' war paint
This ain't no battle scar concealer
I wear my mistakes loud, like I'm royalty
Princess of destroying the patriarchy
I'm not wearing purple lipstick for anybody but me
Because it makes me feel like
Zenon girl of the motherfucking 21st century
I am always two steps ahead
Living in the future
In a world where everyone is less concerned with
the threatening color of my lipstick today
And more concerned with the havoc of my lips
Y'see we women are storm conjurers
and Bruja beauty
We are strength like you've never seen
When you chain us to your societal standards and your
fear of all that we could become
Remember the only one stronger than Sampson
was Delilah
Remember we are accustomed to bleeding
and never giving up the fight
Remember we are royalty
in every ombre, contour, highlight and matte
Remember we were never doing any of this *for you.*

{SUPPERTIME}

I saw *Little Shop of Horrors* for the first time
when I was 11
From then on,
Dentists were always the real villains
Rick Moranis, in all his good guy, cute nerd glory, was the
model for every crush I would ever have
And Ellen Greene
was the only Disney princess I would ever need
Strutting about her *Leave it to Beaver* kitchen
Complete with ruffled lace apron and cartoon blue jays
tying a sweet little bow in the back
Cuddling on the couch with her sweater vest sweetheart
All TV dinners and Lucy in black and white
just before 9:15

> *"A picture out of Better Homes and Gardens*
> *magazine,*
> *Far from Skid Row,*
> *I dream we'll go somewhere that's green,"*

This moment, idyllic in my memory
juxtaposed next to the grim reality of the truth
That Skid Row could swallow you whole if you let it
There is no such thing as a Disney princess here
Instead,
Womanhood comes equipped with
the pepper spray your dad gave you on your 16th birthday,
Headlines about star athletes who walk away unscathed
as you rot, unconscious, legs peeled open
pants down behind a dumpster
It is being "grabbed by the pussy,"
Womanhood is plagued with "yes, sir," and "no, sir,"

and only speaking when spoken to
The idea that Audrey should dream so simply about
> *"a little street in a little suburb...*
> *where everybody has the same little lawn out front*
> *and the same little flagstone patio outback,"*

All the while,
Hitched to a motorcycle with a license plate that reads,
"ABUSE"
Letting the Dentist play Daddy Patriarchy to her
subservient woman
His slap on her cheek echoes
like hundreds of years of systematic oppression
In that moment,
>   I remember the first time a man hit me

I remember playing out my Donna Reed fantasies
in the half-room kitchen of his studio apartment
Pretending to cook when there was no food to eat
Feeling like all I had left were simplistic daydreams
Like my own merit had been buried
Beneath the sting his palm left after striking my face
Knowing there was no mean green motha from outer space
Coming to take him away and swallow him up
Hoping that maybe something would come and swallow
me up instead
I always wondered
why they changed the ending of *Little Shop* for the movie
Now I know
It was because watching that flytrap gulp Audrey up whole
would have been too honest
Because abuse is the real villain
That makes us think our savior is
whatever will swallow us away from this world first

That we deserve to obey or die
Clenching our teeth and fighting
the best way we know how
        If you have ever come face to face
        with Audrey Two
        You have realized
        That the most horrifying thing in the world is
        thinking you would *literally* give your life
        to be anywhere but here
        You slip into the trap's toothy maw
        You succumb to its hunger
        Suddenly,
        You are one with everything you feared
        Finally resting somewhere that's green
This world is eat or be eaten
and the word woman is so often synonymous with
                                    supper

{I AM CHOICE}

The walls of the waiting room are covered in sunset mural
Small town kaleidoscope
A sky view of all that is forgotten once you are called to
the other side of the clinic door
On the other side,
Everything is a painful sterile white
The nurses' questions ring in your ear
Call it dog whistle
Your fear is as evident as the judgment
that lies just outside these glass doors
Abortion is a multiple choice question
in which you choose which way you'd rather die

    a. By succumbing to your own emptiness
         The space you will fill with guilt
         because nothing else will fit there
    b. By living a lie
         The kind that makes its home
         in the eyes of your child
         Every time you make another sacrifice
         Every time you say, "I love you"
    c. Death by hate stare
         from every opinion-bloated judgment junkie
         who thinks they know better
         Who has never had to make a choice like this
         Whose greatest sacrifice
         is not even a morsel of the full plate
         you must force down your throat
         Begging yourself to swallow
         past the dam of tears in your gullet

This was no childhood "choose your own adventure"
No slumber party rendition of *Screw, Marry, Kill*
you have ever dreamed up
Screw: finishing school and following your dreams
Marry: A life of motherhood you were not ready for
Kill: any chance you had of doing more than becoming
another link in the chain
that holds us to this broken system
The world only wants me if I am
Wife
Mother
Winner of the Miss Nuclear Family pageant
Don't they see that the pages of that
Betty Crocker cookbook went up in smoke
The day we women decided to light their
heteronormative housewife horror story on fire?
The day we dedicated ourselves to raising our voices
until someone listens?
The day we felt the flames inside of us
burning their way out?
I am not ***wife***
Or ***mother***
Or playing house for any husband
I am fearless
I am *warrior*
I am *woman*
I am ***C H O I C E***
I am all of the endless possibilities
you could ever dream of
The best
      Doctor
          Teacher
    Lawyer

             Professor
      Bruja
             Poeta
         Mujer
The best anything and everything you've ever seen
I am a world changer, ceiling shatterer,
bright comet leaving my message streaked across the sky
Maybe someday, you can call me *wife* or **mother**
But never resign yourself to thinking
that is all that I am or all I ever will be
Because my options span so much farther
than your normative negativity
I am a *mermaid*
I am the *moon*
I am an entire *galaxy*
I am whatever I goddamn please
I am not a mistake, not a receptacle for your hate
I am **woman**
I am *C H O I C E*
Without choice I cease to exist
Y'see you can't have one without the other because I am
all voice and no silence
I am an *echo*
And I promise
you will be listening to me for a long time

{NOTES ON THE FEMALE AESTHETIC}

My aesthetic is hipster sundress
Winged eyeliner and vinyl Barbra Streisand
It is olive skin and auburn hair
Natural,
Soft and sweet
My aesthetic is a crooked row of bottom teeth
Hidden beneath big brown girl lips
Hips that learned not to lie from Shakira
Only truth
Flat feet, small hands, writer's fork palms
My aesthetic is green chile chicken enchiladas and
My grandmother's smile
while watching *I Dream of Jeannie*
On TV Land for the 178th time
It is home and heart and watermelon sunset
My aesthetic is *beauty*
Please tell me why these boys
Never seem to understand
        Them,
With their sticky fingers
And catcalls
And lack of all decency
To them my aesthetic is
Quiet, easily targeted, and pretty enough
I am double D, short skirt, hourglass waist
Soft, tempting enough to break
My aesthetic is bent over, open mouthed
Porn girl taking direction
It is sad Lana Del Rey

Pepsi Cola Pussy and blue Daisy Dukes girl
Choker around my neck makes it ok
to call me a whore girl
Yell at me from your car window girl
Baby girl, pretty girl,
get in the passenger seat girl,
My aesthetic is
follow me to my next class
Stalk me through the window
while I call campus police girl
Scared to walk down the street
Scared to breathe, scared to think girl
Slow down your motorcycle to ask for a blowjob
Don't stop when I say no girl
Put your hands wherever you want
without my permission girl
Cover up the bruises
So my mama doesn't notice them when I come home
She will always notice them when I come home
I am that girl
Pressed up against the desk at the FedEx
Grabbed at the hips by a drunk man
And escorted out by a kind stranger who says,
"I have a daughter
and wouldn't want her walking out here alone,"
And even then
I cannot trust him simply because of his maleness
I am that girl
Whose legs were opened for the first time
Without a "yes" ever escaping my lips
Ripped,
bleeding,
S h i t

He looked over at the end
Saw my wet, sad face
I will never forget the look in his eyes when he said,
"Stop crying. You're making me feel like an asshole,"
My aesthetic is harassment and abuse and fear
It is that of almost every woman in these United States
In this goddamn world
I pray for my dainty lace glove sister
I know she comes from a long line of survivor women
Who never stopped saying no
Even when the yes's were ripped from their throats
I can still feel his fucking hands on my throat
Sometimes,
I think it is a miracle that I let anyone love me at all
It is a miracle that my body has not been taken from me
more times than this
What sickening things to have to be grateful for
In this world,
We are small and shriveled
Even our deadened insides look like an invitation
Still pretty, still alive enough
My heart is still beating
       So I guess you could say
       My aesthetic is hurt
       My aesthetic is that I was "asking for it"
       It is me crushed beneath the hands of every man
       I will ever meet
       My aesthetic is fear
       It is being afraid
       It is always being afraid
       the grip I cannot escape
       The breath I will always lose
       My aesthetic is woman

My aesthetic is fear
My aesthetic is his hands

{ON LOVE}

{BROOKLYN}

Every time I look at you,
I see Brooklyn
brown eyes blinking; my addiction
I can't stop coming back
for the daisy filled suitcases in the sidewalk cracks
of your sentences
and the moonlit cobblestone walks I fantasize
every time you reach for my hand
I daydream the outline of your arms wrapped around me
the way the number six subway holds the city
tight and precious, like its crown jewel
your smile emulates Times Square at 2 A. M.
      the inside of a star
a man-made moonrise I wish I could excavate forever
the way our bodies find their way around each other
and back like city maps
New York technicolor veins pumping down to the
heartbeat of the shaking subway platform
we ride like we're late
pressed close like a crowded train
you've memorized my route and gone through all the stops
bumping and grinding to these slow floating moments of
Manhattan magic
make love to me like midnight on the Brooklyn bridge
I see the reflection of the neon city on the water
I see the reflection of my eyes in your eyes
and in that moment I can't help but feel like
this is where I belong
My past is a graffiti'd Queens station
some people might look at me

and call me trashy and trampled
trouble scrawled across my rib cage in dull colors
I only see beauty
a mosaic of mistakes turned Michelangelo
every wrong turn, another color on an artist's canvas
you turned my bad tattoos into butterflies
read my spray paint tags
like the instruction manual to my heart
made my yesterdays into a work of art
when you kiss me, I see New Year's Eve confetti
dotting my dreams
my sanctuary city
safe haven of living poems
even the streetlights dance
Somehow, when I'm with you
I don't need a plane ticket to be there
because I'm already in my favorite place in the entire
world
you're the escalator up to 42nd street
the beginning of a bombastic Broadway overture
thin crust pizza and the best fucking mac & cheese
I've ever tasted
you're the first time I stood on top of the galaxy
and saw the whole world shining
you are a little piece of my dreams
tucked away in my suitcase and brought home
to remind me of this starlight glistening life that lies ahead
come back with me and kiss me on the urban Milky Way
let me see the city reflected in your eyes
and your love reflected in your words
watch me trip over the uneven concrete
just so I can say I fell for you
Even if we're not actually there,

I hope you'll see the bright lights in my eyes when I look
at you
and feel my fast city heartbeat when you hold me close
I hope you'll spend any Friday night with me and let it
slowly sink into forever
I hope you'll realize
New York is wherever I'm with you

{I MET YOU ON TINDER}

I met you on Tinder
Made the life changing decision to swipe right
To find out if that was a sparkle in your eye
or just mad screen glare
I'd wait anxiously for your occasional word bubble;
message in a bottle floating across the internet ocean
Your picture reminded me of James Dean
And your little blue words reminded me of
Cry Baby Walker meets Ernest Hemingway
I'm a sucker for existentialism before the first date
In this day and age,
You associate my name with a buzz in your pocket
And my voice with a toneless set of typed observations
sent to your screen
Before you even look into my eyes
You trust that I would never pretend to be someone else
without even meeting me
Before you trust the way you feel when our hands
finally touch for the first time
We are defined by the chat bloop emoji message magic
we use to create ourselves
My Apple heartbeat telling Siri
to start my puppy love playlist when you kiss me
Brain googling why my lips
are caramel lip-gloss sticky afterward every time
Then the next thing I know,
You wanna share a Netflix account
Like, seriously…?
We're not close enough for you to know
that I only ever watch *Friends* re-runs

and serial killer movies
As if trust suddenly means sharing Iphone passwords
and e-mail passwords
and the back-up passwords to your passwords
Can't we just be honest?
No, you can't have my password
Because I'm totally terrified
that you will FIND. MY. PORN.
Suddenly, trust is somehow rooted to
this palm computer box we cater to like a phantom limb
A remote for our emotions
Has anyone ever noticed that all of a sudden
dating means texting 24/7?
And that back in the olden days texting used to be talking
We're always wondering how our grandparents have
stayed together
And it's probably because they didn't talk to each other
ALL THE TIME
Most days, my own brain is quieter than my phone
Most days I need to appreciate the beauty
of being on my own
Constant contact makes it so easy for together
to feel like alone
And makes us unable to see the difference
Constantly immersed in the idea that
Love is a facebook relationship status
That affection is 20 texts to the minute
That trust is having no privacy whatsoever
That the smallest lack of connection is no connection at all
I want unplugged love
Give me the opposite of artificial heartbeat
I want to start out like our grandparents did
When dancing was sex

and sex was truly cherishing body and soul
None of this dick pic touch your clit to me bullshit
I want face to face eye contact til' it's uncomfortable
Smother me with the sound of your voice
The tamber of your laughter
Your infectious inflection
I want to feel your skin like a trail of nervous goosebumps
And speak and smile and kiss with our mouths
instead of our qwerty keyboards
Attach the detached and put the rest of the world on silent
Charging in the back room
So it's just me and you
I don't want our memories to be Instagram
I don't need a billion tiny heart-eyed winky faces
to tell you how I feel
Don't need to shout it from the Zuckerberg rooftops
No googling your name when I miss you
Or twittering my twitterpation
I just want to live in anticipation of the next time I see you
The smell of your favorite coffee
accompanied by your arms around my waist
The way your eyes write Fitzgerald fodder
and I read myself more beautiful
than I ever could've dreamed
The way your cigarette smoke disperses
like droves of unfinished sentences
Your words floating in the recesses of my mind
Lingering in the smell of my t-shirt
Living in the moment you kiss me
like we were looking for an end but we found a beginning
I want to *live* these moments
Full and luminous
So that my life is always too much to text.

{LOVE POEMS, BARS AND OTHER THINGS THAT DON'T GO TOGETHER}

My friend asked me why I never read love poems in bars
and I said, "because people in bars hate love poems"
Bars are the quintessential "leave me the fuck alone,"
place or "fuck me because I'm alone," place
the heartbreak hotel slurred word break-up haven
Where the bartender will always love you
and your beer will never cheat on you
Trust issues do not exist between your lips
and the brim of a tall glass of hoppy hope
You will never accidentally find your IPA on Tinder
or be led on for months by your brew
only to be told
> *"woah...this was nothing serious...*
> *we were just...having a good time"*
I don't read love poems at bars because of people like you
Guy on the barstool
who is looking at me like he wants to street fight me
in the parking lot
for telling all these people the exact reason
he's sitting at this bar tonight
already on his third drink with a shitty look on his face
I know that deep down inside, you guys are all sensitive,
y'know?
you're gonna go home
and eat 12 Reese's peanut butter cups
and watch *The Notebook* after this poem
We get each other
because sometimes,

you just don't need to be reminded of all the orgasms
everyone else is having
you feel like if you see one more couple
go facebook official, you'll go goddamn postal
sometimes you just wanna grab that couple
sitting there with all that hand-holding nose-touching
gross cute bullshit
and concuss them both by slamming their heads together
in a massive collision of *fuck you*
And telling them to go fuck each other
because it's only a matter of time
before they can only go fuck themselves
Alone
In their separate fucking lonely ass apartments
And as you watch the girl start to cry
and the guy trying to mop up his insane nosebleed
you still feel incomplete
because you know that even the pain you've caused
is incomparable to how much it hurts
every time your mind drifts
and you end up thinking about
how much you miss her smile
or the way he used to tell really stupid jokes
and repeat the punchline until it was funny
until you remember the moment that you counted to three,
totally prepared to jump
and he stayed behind with your parachute in his hands
because fear becomes so much stronger than love
Every time you have to peel yourself back up again
after the fall
not everyone knows how to be so open
We are scab pickers
never letting ourselves heal all the way

but so ready to be all clean slate heart
if we had a bicep tattoo,
it would say benefit of the doubt
because we will always give it
even when we are empty
until we're stuck in this Sisyphus cycle
that always puts us right back here
sitting in this exact spot
disappointed, jaded, and somewhat murderous
so, no
I'm not going to read you a *Romeo and Juliet*,
ragged romance,
"you'll find it when you're not looking" love poem
but I will remind you
that you put on clothes today
you made your way to this moment
you are listening
and breathing
and your heart still beats to facilitate
the busy highways of your veins
blood to brain
there's an entire bright lights, big city blood party
inside of you
and you are always invited
trust me
someday someone is gonna hear the bass bumping
under your skin
and knock on your heart's aorta door
with a six pack and a smile
and you'll look into their eyes and tell them
"y'know,
you remind me of this poem I heard at a bar once."

{HIS LIPS}

For you. For the week we spent inside of a magic spell.
This will always be for you.

His lips are a revolution
They are more fires than you could ever hope to put out
Embers dancing like fireflies in the dark night of his pupils
I am lost here
With no map and no want for one
His lips taste like poetry
       And my favorite flavor of ice cream
          And the moment things
              started making sense
Like cigarette smoke and good sex
And laughter that is almost a better indulgence
than the rest
His lips taste like Batman
finally noticing the insignia I put in the sky for him
Soft outlines calling his name and waiting
Saving the day with a side of danger and adventure
low growling voices
Call me Catwoman
Preferably, Michelle Pfeiffer Catwoman
Those lips make me want to purr and pounce
To purse my cherry red pout
Only in the hopes that he cannot resist
I know that I cannot resist
His lips are all the things I ever hoped lips would be
In my 22 years of life,
my lips have never met anyone like him
With all that safe and sound

in his big Brooklyn bridge hands
I know I will not fall
I know that he is there to catch me
  To hold me up till I **stand**
While I watch the pretty lights dance with the city skyline
In the reflection on the water
He says that holding my hand is like dancing
We both take turns leading and following
And I know, just as I stop to listen
The music is in his lips
Y'see those lips are like knowing
you are human-ing so hard
That your heart has decided to throw a block party
like seeing *The Breakfast Club* for the first time
Walking away
Fist through the air
Knowing that you have lived the best way you know how
Like 80's movie montaging all the pieces of your life
together
And knowing that his lips are the best part
of the whole fucking movie
This remarkable being
Blockbuster
Technicolor Jake Ryan reality
Beautiful human
Speaking
  And smiling
    And kissing
      And meaning
        every goddamn
          minute of it
His lips are like knowledge
The forbidden fruit I will continue to suckle and bite

Until I taste all of his truth
Blissfully awake

{ON SURVIVAL}

{BRIAN}

My brother is 15 years old
Wears a size 11 in Women's shoes
And is two high notes away from his first Tony Award
He belts *Rent* in the shower and orders Playbills on Ebay
When he hands out postcards
for his latest community theatre masterpiece,
He is all dates and times
and toothy Broadway marquis smile
The kids in his Biology class don't burn so bright
They shatter the glass bulbs of his iridescent eyes
To them his stage bio reads "gay kid" and "faggot"
To them his voice sounds like a change
they do not know how to comprehend
They'd rather spit and laugh
throwing words at him like rotten tomatoes
Seeds rooting
Blooming into anger and sad Saturday nights
Brian was thirteen years old
the first time he saw *The Rocky Horror Picture Show*
He was all glitter and fishnets, neon and confetti cannons
Makeup smudged to the brink of beauty
        He still is
And I can see it in the way he dreams
He dreams just like my brother
In a stratosphere that only some
could ever hope to get tickets to
It is always sold out
I want my brother to grow up like Brian
To grow up and know that sometimes

people won't like the way your big ambitions and stardust
taste in their mouth
that sometimes
they won't understand
all of the rainbow prism complexities of your beauty
when those lights hit you
that sometimes
they'll throw tomatoes
But you will always be
that disco RuPaul Freddie Mercury
bass heartbeat in the distance
unwavering and effervescent
you will always be that light over at the Frankenstein Place
you will always be a dreamer with dreams
that nobody will ever understand
because to you they're not dreams,
they're motherfuckin plans
because at the end of the day,
we're all a little wild and untamed,
we're all outside in the rain, we're going home
but before we get there,
let's be like Brian and my brother
and remember that these days were made for creation
that now is not the time to dream it, but to be it.

{NORTH STARR}

For my sister. Don't stop shining. We need you.

My sister is a fighter
I never doubted it
Whether I was pinned beneath the grip
of her tiny nail-polished hobbit hands
Or begging for mercy with an arm twisted behind my back
This girl puts up her dukes like motherfucking Rambo
Tasked with waking her up for school every day,
I prepared myself for a WWE Hulk-Hogan-style beating
The Hermia to my Helena,
"Though she be but little, she is fierce,"
All five feet and four inches of her
made out of pure muscle and terror
I always used to say I'd pity the boy
who found his way into the ring with her
She is fucking beautiful
They line up to take her punches
"It's worth it," they say
For a glimpse at that Princess Mononoke glimmer
in her big anime eyes
And the galaxy far, far away in her smile
My sister is a knockout in every sense of the word
She is part Holly Holm, part Rolling Stones,
part Marilyn Monroe
She will kick you clear out of this stratosphere
With her red puckered lips
and heels high enough to take a quick step up to heaven
Did I mention she's only seventeen?
So quit staring, asshole!

To answer the questions your eyes are asking,
Yes, she has always been a Ginger Rogers foxtrot
mixed with a punch like Ali
"Float like a butterfly, sting like a bee,"
But to me, she will always be baby sister
The Amy Pohler to my Tina Fey
The Starr to my moon
Some days, I call her monsoon
The clouds come from out of nowhere
It is raining and raining
no matter how many umbrellas I open
I call my mother stormchaser
Never giving up on trying to tame what she cannot control
Sometimes the storms are bigger than us both
My sister says she will not finish high school
Because she cannot stomach
the passing period whispers of her name
Followed by "slut," and "bitch," and mean ugly sad
She thinks I do not recognize the way her hands shake
from picking up a blade too many times
As if I've never passed through that very
suburb of sadness
Or witnessed its emptiness; queen of a ghost town
I tell her, baby girl,
I made my residence there a long time ago
Here are all the words I have
North Starr,
you must continue to be the brightest in the sky
If you stop shining, we will all be lost
You are a fighter
They have not forced you to the mat yet
Don't give up
Never let go of the Bruce Lee dragon-fire in your soul

And the big deep Frida Kahlo colorful
that lives in your heart
Take no prisoners
You are all three Powerpuff Girls
if they were directed by Quentin Tarantino
Kill Bill meets *Breakfast at Tiffany's*
You are a Hit Girl, Black Widow, Pokemaster Misty
tea party
You can defeat literally anything
Let all the monsters of your depression and anxiety
challenge you to Mortal Kombat
Let a Greta Garbo grin spread across your face
As you serve up a big heaping platter of...K.O.!
Suckerpunching your fears and doubts
And hitting your heartache right where it hurts
as the crowd shouts, "FINISH HER!"
You use the last of that can of whoop ass
you've been saving
Everything you got
We knew you had it in you
Your enemy, lifeless on the ground
You can do it
Stop living in virtual reality
Get out there and kick life in the dick
Re-write *Rocky*
Make it about the day you reclaimed
your big firework smile
Let the ref hold your gloved fist high
And for the first time in a long time, cry happy tears
This won't be your last fight, I promise
But remember, you can do it
We believe in you
You've won the fight before

{JIMMY}

Jimmy told us about his day
while painting his toenails blue
His face is flawlessly make-up'd but his opinions are not
Jimmy speaks his mind like fear is forgettable
Unimpeachable honesty
When a complaint was made about
the protuberance of his package
during the Rocky Horror Show,
the boy bought chocolate penises
for the entire cast and crew and distributed them
since his "seemed to be such a problem for everyone"
Jimmy *loves* Christmas decorations
Loves the way tinsel and trees always keep their promises
The way the star on top can always get you back home
when you're lost
He was all Happy Birthday, Jesus!
And you were…Jewish
When Jimmy falls in love,
It's more like flying
with no intention of ever hitting the ground
He is not considering the difficulty that lies within
the process of getting back up again
when you kissed him,
his heart did a Gene Kelly-Judy Garland
blockbuster number
you Fred Astaire'd your way into his heart and his home
He let you preen and pay
Let you win scrabble and sex and everything in between
Jimmy thinks that awful means wonderful sometimes
That white horses mean Prince Charmings

That emotional vacancy means counseling
That crying laid out on the bathroom floor means insanity
I want him to know that getting over it is bullshit
And closure is a myth
I want him to know that
We are only one New Year's Eve apart
That heartbreak is the kind of sickness
that hits you like a bus
Knocks you flat on your ass
And leaves you auto-immune to your own emotions
Till your body rejects "I love you" like an allergy
And there's no doctor's note to give to your boss
No letter to say
   "sorry I'm behind,
I'm basically dead inside
There's a lighthouse in my heart and the power is out
I stopped singing because
I'm on a scavenger hunt for my voice
And all the clues just lead me right back to him
I think the map is backwards
I hope the map is backwards"
Jimmy asked you to sleep in the guest bedroom
When he was gone,
You packed his things for him
One last reminder that you were in control
Down to the last sharpie marked cardboard flap
He said you still had his graduation cap
And send you a check for the postage
It was $3.23
You never cashed it
And he knows that he was not meant to be
the San Francisco sunrise
To your New Mexico moon

That he's let himself fall victim to your pull
for far too long
It's all he can do to look for another star
Even though you're still the brightest light in the sky
to him
He can't look up without seeing you
But he'll spend his days reminding himself
that there's still a sky without you
Jimmy gave you a check for everything he had
Heart and soul
Vibrato and vulnerability
His laughter and all of his Saturday nights
You never cashed it

{S U P E R N O V A}

For Andrew. My Supernova. The original M E S S. Always remember that you deserve nothing less than this.

Supernova,
Did you know that the universe begets itself?
That the center of our galaxy smells like raspberries
and tastes like rum
That unless science is just around to fuck with us
We are, all of us,
Made up of a tiny fraction of the same
effervescent glitter dust that makes up the stars

Supernova,
Did you know that the word galaxy is defined as
A system of millions or billions of stars
dancing in the dust that surrounds them
Held together simply by gravitational attraction
That a supernova is a star
that suddenly increases greatly in brightness
because of a catastrophic explosion
Leaving everything in a fog of purple debris moonshine
and technicolor raspberry rum
I know that not long ago,
You thought the definition of the universe was his name
The taste of his tongue
The wisp of his breath on your neck
I want you to know that he's just one star
And maybe you let the gravitational attraction
sweep you up
Until you created a galaxy just for the two of you

Supernova,
> You are the original M E S S
> Look at you
Letting yourself shine like that
I want you to know that as much as it hurts to explode
You were too big for that galaxy anyway
You never belonged with a single star

Supernova,
Did you know there are over 100 billion stars
in our galaxy alone?
You were never destined to blend
into the never-ending black night sky
> No
> Not you
All radio GaGa, sequins in your smile
We could all get drunk on the way that you laugh
On the way that you sing for your life
and live for your dreams
And solve everything with an amaretto sour
And a medium McDonald's french fry
Supernova,
It's okay to burst until you're engulfed in so much glitter
that it just seems like dirt
To feel like the explosion will never end
It's okay
But I want you to know that

You are a supernova and you deserve galaxy

Though you might settle for one star
I want you to know that you deserve 100 billion of them

With Mariah Carey's *"Emotions,"*
playing in the background of your every embrace
While you dance underneath a cataclysmic disco ball of
    "Yaaaassss Queen!"
You deserve the confetti
And the Miss America wave
from the top of your parade float
You deserve serenades
And breakfast on Saturday morning
You deserve love like the moon
  Unfailing
    Remaining through all of its phases
    Everlasting

  You are a supernova and you deserve a galaxy

{ACKNOWLEDGEMENTS}

I would like to thank all of the people who courageously opened their hearts to me and allowed me to re-write all that beauty into poems you can find in this book.

To the boys in these poems, thank you for the beautiful time we shared. Thank you for the heartbreak. I am lucky to have loved the way I've loved.

To Patrick, thank you for your constant support.

To my queen, Andrew, for drunk Amaretto sour nights and crying into McDonald's french fries that all lead to some of my most beautiful memories. I love you.

To Jimmy, for all that big love in your heart. Never stop sharing it.

To Brian, thank you for the Rocky Horror sparkle you bring to the whole world.

To Megan Rader, thank you for constantly believing in me and championing my artistic work. It is because of you that I am willing to take chances no matter the consequences.

To Kathleen Clawson, thank you for giving my words a home. Thank you for making them sing.

To my sister and brothers, I am so lucky to come from a family full of success stories. You are brave and resilient and full of all of the beautiful things in this world.

To Mercedez, Eva, Jessica, and Damien, you inspire me continually, you have helped me grow as an artist and as a person and I love you with my whole bruja heart. B.H. Kisses.

To Bendicto, thank you for being so pretty. Thank you for showing me how pretty I am. I will never watch *Purple Rain* without thinking of you.

To my beautiful friends, I would not be this person if it were not for you. This is for Dustin, Gino, and Juliana. Thank you for being a stained glass piece that makes up the mosaic of my heart.

Lastly, to my parents, thank you for all of your support no matter what crazy thing comes out of my mouth. I am so grateful for your constant love and encouragement. I am so grateful for this voice. I am so grateful. Alabanza. Praise to right now. Praise to this moment.

{ABOUT THE AUTHOR}

GiGi Guajardo//{gigi bella} is an award-winning poet, musical theatre actress, and educator of the arts. She recently earned the title of Albuquerque's Woman of the World 2017 representative. She was named a group piece champion at the 2016 National Poetry Slam and a National Semi-Finalist at the 2013 National Poetry Slam as a member of the Albuquerque Slam Team. She is a student at the University of New Mexico pursuing a bachelor's degree in American Studies with a Theatre minor. She loves marshmallows, sparkling purple lipstick, and Wes Anderson movies. She continues to be a hopeless romantic.

Also available from
Swimming with Elephants Publications, LLC

My Blood is Beautiful
Mercedez Holtry

September
Katrina K Guarascio & Gina Marselle

Cunt.Bomb.
Jessica Helen Lopez

You Must Be This Tall to Ride
SaraEve Fermin

Periscope Heart
Kai Coggin

They Are All Me
Dominique Christina

Find More Publications at:
swimmingwithelephants.com

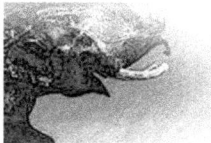